Step 1
Go to www.av2books.com

Step 2
Enter this unique code

ICJEG3N61

Step 3
Explore your interactive eBook!

AV2 is optimized for use on any device

Your interactive eBook comes with...

Contents
Browse a live contents page to easily navigate through resources

Audio
Listen to sections of the book read aloud

Videos
Watch informative video clips

Weblinks
Gain additional information for research

Try This!
Complete activities and hands-on experiments

Key Words
Study vocabulary, and complete a matching word activity

Quizzes
Test your knowledge

Slideshows
View images and captions

This title is part of our AV2 digital subscription

1-Year K–5 Subscription
ISBN 978-1-7911-3320-7

Access hundreds of AV2 titles with our digital subscription.
Sign up for a FREE trial at www.av2books.com/trial

Gardening

FRUITS

CONTENTS

AV2 Book Code	2
All about Fruit	4
Why Plant Fruit?	6
The Life Cycle of a Fruit Tree	8
When to Plant	10
Where to Plant	12
Fruit Farms in the United States	14
Choosing Your Fruit	16
Ready to Plant	18
Fruit Tree Care	20
10-Question Fruit Quiz	22
Key Words/Index	23

All about Fruit

If you were to grow fruit with your mom or dad, what types of fruit would you plant? Why did you choose these ones? Do you like the way they taste? Are they interesting shapes or colors?

Fruit can grow on trees, as well as on other plants, such as **vines**, shrubs, and bushes. Growing your own fruit is a fun way to learn about these different plants. You will discover what they need to grow and produce fruit. Fresh fruit is healthy and delicious!

Fruit tastes best when it is ripe. By growing your own fruit, you can pick it fresh from the plant.

What Is a Fruit?

A fruit is the fleshy part of a plant that has seeds and can be used for food. Fruits have several parts.

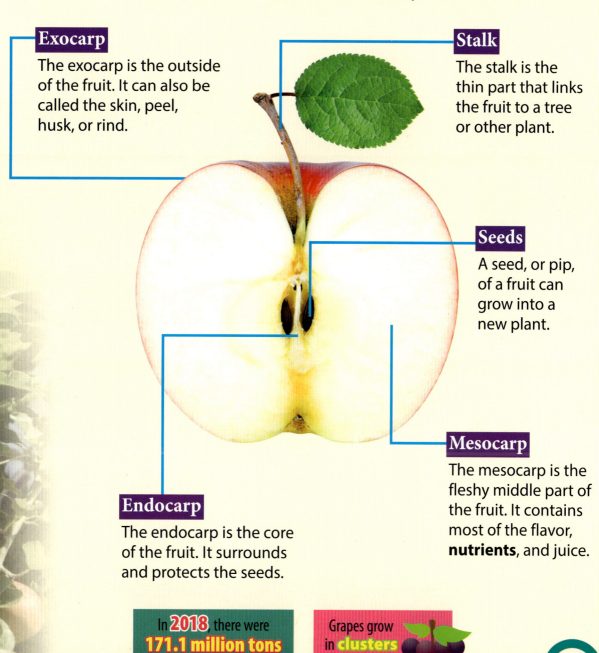

Exocarp
The exocarp is the outside of the fruit. It can also be called the skin, peel, husk, or rind.

Stalk
The stalk is the thin part that links the fruit to a tree or other plant.

Seeds
A seed, or pip, of a fruit can grow into a new plant.

Mesocarp
The mesocarp is the fleshy middle part of the fruit. It contains most of the flavor, **nutrients**, and juice.

Endocarp
The endocarp is the core of the fruit. It surrounds and protects the seeds.

In **2018**, there were **171.1 million tons** of bananas grown worldwide. (155.2 million tonnes)

Grapes grow in **clusters** of about **75 berries** each.

5

Why Plant Fruit?

Fruits add bright pops of color to your yard. Some fruits also smell nice. Fruit plants can make any space more appealing. They are important for other reasons as well.

All fruits come from flowers. Fruit plants are very important because their flowers make a sweet liquid called nectar. Insects such as bees and butterflies land on the flowers to drink the nectar. When they do this, **pollen** sticks to their bodies, then falls off on the next flowers they visit. This helps the flowers make seeds so new plants can grow.

Oranges are high in vitamin C, which can prevent sickness and help people heal faster.

Fruit is a nutritious snack. It contains **fiber** and **vitamins** that help keep people healthy.

Some fruits, such as juniper berries, can be used to make medicine.

The Life Cycle of a Fruit Tree

All fruits begin life, grow, and make more fruits. This is the life cycle of a fruit tree.

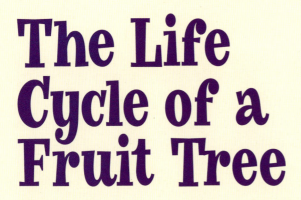

Seed
Some fruits begin life as seeds. A seed will grow once it is planted.

Fruit
Birds and other animals eat the fruit and spread its seeds. The cycle begins again.

Trees
It can take about 6 to 10 years for a tree to grow large enough to start producing fruit.

Flower Bud
Flower buds grow on the branches of a mature tree. In the spring, they **bloom**.

Flowers
Insects and other animals **pollinate** the flowers. Then, the flowers become fruit.

When to Plant

What is the weather like where you live? Is it very hot in the summer? Do you have long winters? Different fruits need certain conditions to grow well.

It is important to plant your fruit at the right time of year. If it is too cold outside, your fruit may not grow. The best time to plant depends on where you live and the kind of fruit you are planting. **Citrus** fruits, such as lemons, limes, and oranges, need hot weather to grow. Grapes and cherries can be planted in cold weather.

If you live somewhere cold, plant your fruit trees early in the spring.

SUMMER

Summer is often called berry season. This is a perfect time to pick fruits such as strawberries, blueberries, raspberries, and blackberries.

WINTER

The seeds of some fruits, such as plums, need time in the cold to get ready to grow.

Strawberries are **one of the healthiest** fruits.

It takes about **three to four years** for a **peach tree** to **grow fruit**.

Where to Plant

It is important that you choose the right place to plant your fruit. How do you know if a place is right? There are three main factors you should consider.

Sun

Your garden should be somewhere that gets sunlight. Research which plants need sunshine all day and which ones prefer shade. Choose areas of your yard that fit the needs of your fruit.

Soil

Plants may get **root rot** if they are left sitting in very wet soil. Make sure to use soil with good **drainage** for your fruit plants.

Wind

Fruit can be damaged by cold winds. If possible, plant your fruit near a fence that will block the wind, but not the sunlight.

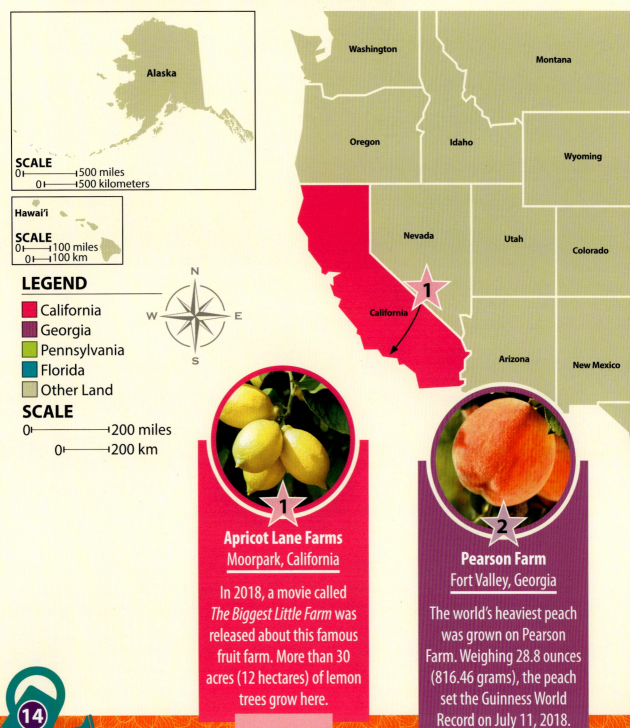

Fruit Farms in the United States

Apricot Lane Farms
Moorpark, California

In 2018, a movie called *The Biggest Little Farm* was released about this famous fruit farm. More than 30 acres (12 hectares) of lemon trees grow here.

Pearson Farm
Fort Valley, Georgia

The world's heaviest peach was grown on Pearson Farm. Weighing 28.8 ounces (816.46 grams), the peach set the Guinness World Record on July 11, 2018.

Many types of fruit are grown in the United States. Certain states are known for the type of fruit they grow, such as Georgia peaches or Florida oranges. Some fruit farms even allow visitors to come and pick their own fruit.

Weaver's Orchard
Morgantown, Pennsylvania

Weaver's Orchard grows more than 30 kinds of apples. A new apple variety called the Star Gala was discovered here in 1995.

King Ranch
South Bay, Florida

King Ranch is the largest juice orange producer in the country. Valencia and other juice oranges make up about 91 percent of its yearly harvest.

Choosing Your Fruit

Fruits come in many different colors and textures. Some fruits taste sour, while others are sweet. How do you choose which ones you should plant? One of the first things to consider is where you will grow your fruit. Does your yard have enough space for a large fruit tree to grow? Would smaller fruit plants be a better fit for you? Also consider how much time you want to invest. Caring for some fruit plants takes more time than others.

Planting berries is one of the best ways to attract birds to your yard.

Trees
Fruit trees require plenty of space and time to produce fruit. They also take the most work to grow.

Cherry Tree

Peach Tree

Plum Tree

Grape Vine

Blackberry Shrub

Vines, Shrubs, and Bushes
Many small fruit plants are easy to maintain. Berries often grow quickly and require less patience to care for than fruit trees.

Blueberry Bush

Ready to Plant

If you want to grow fruits, you have to start with the right equipment. You also have to follow the planting process.

Gardening Equipment

Shovel
Use a shovel to dig holes when planting your fruit trees. You can also use a shovel to spread **mulch**.

Hose
Fruit plants need water to grow. Use a hose to keep your plants from getting too dry if it does not rain.

Stake
Some plants need help to stand. A stake is a wooden stick that you can tie your plants to for support, if necessary.

The Planting Process

1. Use your shovel to dig a hole for your fruit tree. The hole should be two times as wide as the **root ball**.

2. Spread the roots out and place the tree in the hole. Then, use your shovel to refill the hole with soil.

3. Use your hose to water the soil well.

4. If needed, stake the tree so it stands straight.

5. Use your shovel to cover the ground around the tree with mulch.

Repeat for each fruit tree you want to plant.

Fruit Tree Care

Taking care of fruit trees does not stop with planting. It can take years to grow fruit trees. You must check on them every day to make sure that your fruit is growing and staying healthy. There are three main areas that could need attention.

Moisture

Water your fruit tree well, especially during dry weather. Cover the ground around the tree with mulch to prevent the water from drying up.

Nutrients

Fertilizer will give your fruit tree the nutrients it needs to grow. One year after planting, add fertilizer to the soil around your tree.

Space

Trees need space for their leaves and fruit to grow. Prune, or cut off, some branches from your fruit tree to give other branches enough space.

10 Question Fruit Quiz

1 What is the outside of a fruit called?

2 In what kind of weather can grapes and cherries be planted?

3 What may happen if a plant's roots sit in very wet soil?

4 Why should you prune your fruit trees?

5 What makes fruit healthy for people to eat?

6 What famous fruit farm was the subject of the movie *The Biggest Little Farm*?

7 Why should you plant your fruit near a fence, if possible?

8 Why should you use mulch?

9 Where was the Star Gala apple discovered?

10 Which tool can be used to dig holes for your fruit plants and to spread mulch?

ANSWERS 1. Exocarp **2.** In cold weather **3.** It can get root rot **4.** To give other branches space to grow fruit **5.** Fiber and vitamins **6.** Apricot Lane Farms in Moorpark, California **7.** To prevent your fruit from being damaged by the wind **8.** To prevent the water from drying up around your tree **9.** Weaver's Orchard in Morgantown, Pennsylvania **10.** A shovel

Key Words

bloom: when a mature flower produces a colorful head to attract pollinators

citrus: a kind of tree or shrub producing juicy, pulpy flesh in a thick rind, such as lemon or orange

drainage: the removal of water from soil

fertilizer: a mixture that adds nutrients to soil

fiber: a material that helps move food through the digestive tract

mulch: material, such as decaying leaves or bark, that is spread around or over a plant to enrich or protect the surrounding soil

nutrients: substances that promote growth

pollen: a dust made by plants that helps them develop seeds

pollinate: to carry plant dust from one plant to another so seeds can be made

root ball: the tight ball of roots and soil formed by a sapling

root rot: a condition in which a plant's roots start to decay

vines: climbing or trailing plants that grow long, spreading stems

vitamins: organic substances, which must be included in a healthy diet to aid in proper growth and nutrition

Index

Apricot Lane Farms 14, 22

bushes 4, 17

color 4, 6, 16

equipment 18

fertilizer 21
flower bud 9
flowers 6, 9

hose 18, 19

insects 6, 9

King Ranch 15

leaves 21

mulch 18, 19, 20, 22

nutrients 5, 21

Pearson Farm 14
pollination 6, 9

root 13, 19, 22

seeds 5, 6, 8, 11
shovel 18, 19, 22
shrubs 4, 17
soil 13, 19, 21, 22
stake 18, 19
sunlight 12, 13

trees 4, 5, 8, 9, 10, 11, 14, 16, 17, 18, 19, 20, 21, 22

vines 4, 17

water 18, 19, 20, 22
Weaver's Orchard 15, 22
wind 13, 22

Get the best of both worlds.

AV2 bridges the gap between print and digital.

The expandable resources toolbar enables quick access to content including **videos**, **audio**, **activities**, **weblinks**, **slideshows**, **quizzes**, and **key words**.

Animated videos make static images come alive.

Resource icons on each page help readers to further **explore key concepts**.

Published by AV2
276 5th Avenue
Suite 704 #917
New York, NY 10001
Website: www.av2books.com

Copyright ©2022 AV2
All rights reserved. No part of this publication may be reproduced, stored in a retrieval system, or transmitted in any form or by any means, electronic, mechanical, photocopying, recording, or otherwise, without the prior written permission of the publisher.

Library of Congress Cataloging-in-Publication Data
Names: Noelle, Becky, author.
Title: Fruits / Becky Noelle.
Description: New York, NY : AV2, [2022] | Series: Gardening | Includes index. | Audience: Grades 2-3
Identifiers: LCCN 2020022325 (print) | LCCN 2020022326 (ebook) | ISBN 9781791127671 (library binding) | ISBN 9781791127688 (paperback) | ISBN 9781791127695 (ebook other) | ISBN 9781791127701 (ebook other)
Subjects: LCSH: Fruit--Juvenile literature.
Classification: LCC SB357.2 .N64 2021 (print) | LCC SB357.2 (ebook) | DDC 634--dc23
LC record available at https://lccn.loc.gov/2020022325
LC ebook record available at https://lccn.loc.gov/2020022326

Printed in Guangzhou, China
1 2 3 4 5 6 7 8 9 0 25 24 23 22 21

022021
101120

Editor: Katie Gillespie
Art Director: Terry Paulhus

Every reasonable effort has been made to trace ownership and to obtain permission to reprint copyright material. The publisher would be pleased to have any errors or omissions brought to its attention so that they may be corrected in subsequent printings. AV2 acknowledges Getty Images, iStock, Shutterstock, and Dreamstime as its primary image suppliers for this title.